ROLLING SMOOTH - FROM BREAKDOWNS TO BELLY LAUGHS

Stan Cromlish

Copyright © 2025 Stan Cromlish

All rights reserved.

ISBN: 978-1-945838
ISBN-13: 978-1-945838-06-4

This book is dedicated to everyone who dreams of chasing Brother Highway in an RV and refuses to take "no" for an answer. To the wanderers who see freedom in the distance and go after it anyway.

To my Mom and Dad, who may not have always shared my vision but always gave me the space to find it. Your patience, love, and quiet support have been the compass that's kept me rolling smooth.

And to every traveler at heart—may your journey be bold, your road kind, and your laughter loud along the way.

CONTENTS

Foreword 1

Chapter One 4

Chapter Two 8

Chapter Three 18

Chapter Four 27

Chapter Five 38

Chapter Six 52

Chapter Seven 59

Chapter Eight 67

Foreword

Well, hello there. My name's Bessie, though if you've read much of Stan's work, you already know that. I'm a 2013 Forest River Sunseeker 2300, and I had the honor—and let me emphasize the *ordeal*—of being Stan's very first motorhome. I was the training wheels, the guinea pig, the crash test dummy for everything he thought he knew about RVing... and everything he didn't.

Now, don't get me wrong, I'm proud of my place in his story. Every RVer needs that first rig—the one that bears the brunt of their learning curve. I just didn't realize when he bought me that I'd be starring in so many of his "what-not-to-do" adventures. If you ever wondered what it's like to live with a new RVer behind the wheel, buckle up.

Let's start with the power. Oh, the power. Stan had a lot of enthusiasm, but his understanding of amps, volts, and breakers was, to say the least, *developing*. I remember the time he decided to run the microwave, the coffee pot, and the air conditioner all at once. One second, I was humming along, lights glowing, AC buzzing; the next, *click*—darkness. He looked at me like I'd failed him, but trust me, it wasn't me. That's when he learned the difference between 30 amps and wishful thinking.

And then there was the awning incident. Oh yes, that one's burned into my memory. We were staying at the Alsatian RV Resort in Texas, and Stan, bless him, forgot to bring in my awning before pulling out of the gate. I tried to tell him—honest, I did. I rattled and creaked like an old screen door in a windstorm, but he didn't listen. Next thing I knew, my beautiful awning arm was tangled up with a gatepost, and the gatepost won. The sound of metal on metal isn't pretty, let me tell you.

He looked back in horror, I groaned in pain, and we both learned that awnings are not optional accessories—they're fragile appendages that require respect.

Don't get me started on his obsession with water. At first, he didn't trust a single drop that came out of campground spigots. He lugged around five-gallon jugs of bottled water like we were crossing the Sahara. Then, when he finally did trust the hookups, he had no idea how temperamental a black tank could be. Let's just say there were times when I felt like a science experiment gone wrong. The good news? He eventually figured out filters, flushes, and that little dance every RVer does when they're praying the sensors aren't lying.

Traveling with Stan also meant adventures on the open road—some smoother than others. I'll never forget pulling into those tiny campsites where I barely fit, like a linebacker trying to squeeze into a child's booster seat. He'd inch me forward, back me up, get out, wave his arms, scratch his head, and then do it all again. Sometimes the neighbors would pull up a chair just to watch the show. If there'd been popcorn, we could have sold tickets.

Now, don't think I'm complaining. Stan may have been green, but he treated me with love. He gave me a name, after all. Not every rig gets that kind of respect. He washed me, waxed me, and even when I carried the scars of his learning curve, he never blamed me outright. He just shook his head, muttered something about lessons learned, and promised to do better next time. And eventually, he did.

I like to think I prepared him for Bertha and then Bertie Bea. By the time he moved on, he understood more about weight, tires, leveling, and all the quirks that make an RV tick. I was the one who bore the brunt of his rookie mistakes, but I was also the one who gave him the confidence to keep going.

And here's the thing: every dent, every scratch, every black tank mishap turned into a story. That's what you're holding in your hands right now—those stories. In the moment, they were frustrating, sometimes even a little scary. But with time, they've become the kind of tales that make you laugh until your sides hurt.

* * *

So, as you dive into this book, just remember: RV life isn't about perfection. It's about rolling with the punches, learning from the breakdowns, and finding humor in the hiccups. If I, Bessie, could survive Stan's early days of RVing, then you can survive just about anything the open road throws at you.

And who knows? Maybe one day, you'll look back at your own rookie mistakes with the same belly laughs. Until then, sit back, turn the page, and enjoy the ride. I know I did.

—Bessie
 Stan's Faithful First Rig

CHAPTER ONE
Introduction

Welcome to the Chaos

When I first jumped into the RV life, I had no idea what I was doing. None. Zip. Nada. I thought I did, of course—that's the dangerous part. I'd watched a few YouTube videos, read a blog or two, and convinced myself that driving a house on wheels across the country would be no different than driving a U-Haul across town. Spoiler alert: it is *very* different.

My first rig, Bessie, a 2013 Forest River Sunseeker 2300, was the poor soul who had to endure my rookie mistakes. Looking back, she deserves a medal—or at least a retirement plaque. She was the one who taught me what happens when you don't fully understand power management, or when you assume that an RV's awning can somehow withstand a gatepost at the Alsatian RV Resort in Texas. (It can't.) Let's just say, awning arms don't bend gracefully.

Then came Bertha, my 2015 Forest River Sunseeker 3050s. Bigger, bolder, and somehow even more patient with me than Bessie. But she too had her share of battle scars. Like the time in Wyoming when I ran over a cable stretched across the road and it wrapped itself tightly around Rosie, my tow car. Picture me sitting there on the side of the road with Bertha hooked up, Rosie hogtied like a calf at a rodeo, and me pacing like a cowboy who just realized he roped the wrong steer. Hours later, roadside assistance arrived to free Rosie from her steel noose, and I had one of those "what in the world am I doing with my life?" moments.

And finally, there's Bertie Bea, my 2016 Tiffin Allegro Open Road 34PA, who's been with me through the most miles, the most rallies, and the most misadventures. By the time she rolled into my life, I had learned a few things—emphasis on *a few*. I knew how to weigh a rig, keep tire pressures dialed in, and even manage power without turning the whole RV into a disco of tripped breakers. But the universe has a funny way of reminding you that just when you think you've got this lifestyle figured out, it throws a thunderstorm in Dodge City, or a parking space so small you swear it was painted by a sadistic campground host.

That's what this book is all about. *Rolling Smooth: From Breakdowns to Belly Laughs* isn't a collection of perfectly filtered Instagram sunsets or Facebook highlight reels where everything goes right and everyone looks glamorous standing next to their rigs. Nope. These are the stories of the other side of RV life—the breakdowns, the blunders, the boneheaded mistakes—that at the time made me want to pull my hair out, but now? Now they make me laugh.

Because here's the truth: if you spend any amount of time on the road in an RV, things will go wrong. Slides won't slide. Awnings will lose to gates (because you forgot to bring them in). Jacks won't jack. And sometimes, it feels like every star in the sky has aligned against you. In those moments, you're not thinking about life lessons or character building. You're wondering if maybe you should sell everything, buy a condo, and take up golf.

But here's the kicker—those are the moments that end up shaping your journey the most. Not because they're fun in the moment (trust me, they're not), but because once the dust settles, once the tow truck leaves, once the awning gets repaired, you realize you survived it. And you usually come away with a pretty good story to tell around the campfire.

This book is my campfire. These chapters are the tales of rookie mistakes, unexpected storms, and campsite mishaps that tested my patience and sometimes my sanity. They're the stories of how Bessie, Bertha, Bertie Bea, and Rosie all earned their scars—and how I learned, usually the hard way, that RV life demands a good sense of humor.

Some of these stories will make you cringe. Others will make you nod in recognition, because you've been there too. And a few might even teach you something useful, though let's be honest—most of what you'll learn is what *not* to do.

So grab a cup of coffee, settle into your favorite chair, and get ready to laugh at my expense. Because if there's one lesson RV life has taught me, it's this: the road is full of surprises, and sometimes the only way to keep rolling smooth is to laugh your way through the breakdowns.

CHAPTER TWO

The Black Tank Blues

If there's one thing that separates RVers from the rest of polite society, it's the black tank. Everyone else goes about their lives never giving a second thought to where things go when they flush. But us? We obsess over it. We debate chemicals, argue about sensors, and swap horror stories like old fishermen talking about "the one that got away."

When I first started RVing in Bessie, my 2013 Forest River Sunseeker 2300, I thought the black tank was just a tank. You fill it, you dump it, you go on with your day. Simple, right? Wrong. That tank had a mind of its own. No matter what I did, the sensors never read "empty." I could drain it until it gurgled like a dying walrus, and the panel would still insist I was half full. At first, I thought maybe I just didn't understand the system. Then I realized I was living with a curse: the permanent Black Tank Blues.

I tried everything people told me. There was the famous "bag of ice" trick, where you dump a bag of ice into the tank, hit the road, and let it rattle around to scrape the insides clean. Folks swore by it. "It'll knock the crud right off those sensors," they said. So one summer day, I bought a bag of ice, dumped it in, and took off. Miles later, I stopped, flushed, and checked the sensors. Still half full. The only thing I had accomplished was melting three dollars' worth of perfectly good ice cubes. I could've cooled a six-pack of beer with that bag, and instead, I sacrificed it to the black tank gods.

And that was just the beginning.

* * *

Bessie wasn't my only teacher. When Bertha came along, I figured I'd learned my lesson. But Bertha, bless her big heart, had her own sense of humor. I remember one time standing there with the hose hooked up, feeling proud of myself for finally having a system down. Gloves on, sewer elbow locked in, flush valve open, water flowing—it was almost like I knew what I was doing. And then... splat. Let's just say the hose wasn't as secure as I thought. Bertha made sure I walked away from that one smelling like I'd lost a bar fight with a porta-john.

By the time Bertie Bea came into my life, I was a veteran. Or so I thought. I had fancier equipment, sturdier hoses, and a smug confidence that comes from surviving a few too many close calls. But even Bertie Bea liked to keep me humble. Sensors lied. Valves stuck. One time, I stood there waiting for the glorious sound of a rushing flush, only to get a trickle. Nothing strikes fear into an RVer's heart faster than realizing the tank you thought was empty... isn't.

And then there are the friends. Ah, yes. RVing is full of opportunities to learn from your own mistakes, but every now and then, you get the privilege of learning from someone else's. I once watched a buddy of mine—who shall remain nameless to protect his dignity—accidentally connect his city water hose to the black tank flush instead of the fresh water inlet. Now, if you're not familiar, the black tank flush is designed to spray water around inside your black tank to clean it out *after* you've emptied it. But if you leave the valve closed and pump water in? Well, congratulations. You've just built a pressurized sewage bomb. This story is in the chapter.

Sure enough, his tank filled up like a balloon until it couldn't take it anymore. The next sound we heard was not unlike a whale breaching —an eruption of biblical proportions. The aftermath required a garden hose, a change of clothes, and a very long shower. I don't think he's ever lived that one down, and honestly, neither should he.

The truth is, every RVer has their own version of the Black Tank Blues. It's a rite of passage. You can read all the guides, buy all the chemicals, and watch all the YouTube videos you want, but at some point, you'll be standing there with a stinky hose in your hand, wondering what life choices brought you to this moment. And when you finally get past the frustration, when the smell fades and the hose is put away, you'll have a story to tell—and usually a pretty funny one.

That's what this chapter is all about. The good, the bad, and the stinky. The times when I thought I had it figured out, only to be humbled by a stubborn sensor or a rogue flush. The near disasters that turned into comedy gold. And yes, the unforgettable moments that taught me, once and for all, that humor is the best deodorizer.

So buckle up—or maybe hold your nose—and come along for the ride. Because nothing says "RV life" quite like the blues that come from a black tank that refuses to play nice.

The Toilet Paper Baseball Incident

August in the Smoky Mountains usually means two things: hot weather and cooler trout streams. So when a couple of my buddies suggested a guys' fishing weekend in Cherokee, North Carolina, I didn't hesitate. Bertie Bea, my trusty 2016 Tiffin Allegro Open Road 34PA, was loaded up and ready to serve as both our cabin and our refuge. We rolled into the Cherokee/Great Smoky Mountains KOA Holiday, found our spot, hooked up to power and water, and settled in.

Now, the fishing wasn't quite what we'd hoped—it rarely is when you start the trip bragging about how good it's *going to be*. Still, we had a blast: casting into the Oconaluftee River, solving the world's problems around a campfire, and arguing over whether trout prefer dry flies or nymphs (for the record, they preferred neither that weekend).

By Sunday, we'd overeaten, fished too little, and laughed plenty. As we packed up, I made one of those decisions that, in hindsight, deserves its own warning label: *I'll dump the tanks later.* My tanks were empty when we arrived, and I figured letting the Kleen Tank cocktail of Pine-Sol and Calgon Bath Pearls slosh around during the drive to Chattanooga would give everything a good cleaning. This is a tried-and-true trick for RVers: a little road motion, a little cleaner, and the black tank comes out sparkling—well, as sparkling as a black tank can get.

What I didn't know was that one of my buddies had apparently decided to use three-quarters of a roll of toilet paper in a single weekend. I don't know if he was practicing papier-mâché projects in the bathroom or if he really likes to be *thorough*, but by the time we hit the road, that mountain of TP had congealed into something roughly the size of a major league baseball. And it was lying in wait, perfectly positioned to ruin my day.

Fast forward a few hours: I pulled into the Chattanooga North/Cleveland KOA, leveled Bertie Bea, hooked up the power, and settled in for a couple of days of work. Feeling productive, I decided to take care of the tanks. I strolled outside, sewer hose in place, gloves on like a surgeon about to perform a delicate operation, and pulled the black tank valve.

At first, everything flowed just fine. Sweet relief, I thought. But then, just as I was beginning to congratulate myself on another successful dump—*thunk*. The flow stopped. Dead. Like a traffic jam on I-40, except smellier.

I walked back inside, checked the sensors, and sure enough: still one-third full. That's when I knew something wasn't right.

I hustled back outside and tried closing the valve. No dice. It wouldn't shut all the way. That's when panic started whispering in my ear. Removing the sewer hose was out of the question—I may be reckless, but I'm not insane. The image of a black tank geyser shooting across my KOA site was enough to keep me firmly on the side of caution.

So there I was: crouched next to Bertie Bea, gate valve jammed open, sewer hose full, and a baseball-sized mystery clog holding everything hostage. I started cussing—at my friends, at my luck, at myself for not just dumping in Cherokee. I even cussed at Bertie Bea, though she's entirely innocent in this saga.

After a few deep breaths and a moment of questioning every life choice that led me here, I decided to get scientific. Step one: add more water. Sometimes, you need a little extra push. I hooked up the hose and started filling the black tank again, praying I wasn't about to create a sewage tsunami. Step two: work the valve back and forth, like a plumber playing tug-of-war with fate.

For two hours, I battled that clog. Water came in, the valve went out.

The valve went in, and water was pushed out. A few trickles managed to seep past, but most of it refused to move. I was sweaty, frustrated, and thinking about calling a priest for an exorcism.

And then, just as suddenly as it began, the baseball let go. With a gurgle and a whoosh that I swear sounded like a victory cheer, the dam burst. Out it came, a tidal wave of toilet paper and tank contents, roaring through the hose and into the sewer like it had been waiting for its big moment.

I jumped back like a man who'd just defused a bomb, feeling both relieved and horrified. The worst was over, but the smell made sure I'd never forget it. I flushed the tank twice more just to be safe, then stood there in triumph, hose hanging like a battle flag after a hard-fought victory.

My buddies had no idea about the ordeal I'd just survived since they had gone home. So naturally, I informed them via a text message—with a bit of friendly shaming for good measure. "Fellas," I texted, "this isn't your grandma's bathroom. You can't just send half a forest down the pipes and hope for the best. More water, less paper—that's the rule."

They laughed. I didn't. Not at first, anyway. But eventually, even I had to admit it was funny. Not in the moment, mind you—but later, when the smell was gone and the crisis was over, it became another story in the growing anthology of *The Black Tank Blues*.

The lesson? RV life will test you, especially when it comes to that most dreaded of tanks. But with patience, persistence, and just a touch of dark humor, you'll make it through. And if you're lucky, you'll come away with a story that makes your friends laugh around the campfire —preferably after you've showered.

Mount Vesuvius at Mountain Cove

For some reason, the summer of 2025 decided to gift me a steady supply of Black Tank Blues. Usually, I only get one or two "memorable" events a year—you know, the kind of disasters you laugh about later, once you've changed clothes and the smell has faded. But this summer? The black tank gremlins were working overtime.

Now, this particular story isn't about *my* black tank—thankfully—but it still left me soaked, smelly, and swearing. And it's a prime example of how the Black Tank Blues have no boundaries. They can strike rookies, veterans, and even those of us who are just innocent bystanders minding our own business.

I had rolled into Mountain Cove Farms Resort in Chickamauga, Georgia, for the 11th Annual Cowboy & Cowgirl Reunion—a weekend full of rodeo stories, cowboy church, and good friends. Bertie Bea was leveled and settled, awning out, chairs in the shade. I had my boots off, a book in hand, and was enjoying one of those rare quiet moments on the road. The only sound was the hum of cicadas and the distant whinny of horses from the stables.

Then my phone buzzed.

It was an old friend, one of those guys you've known long enough that you never hesitate to pick up. He had just pulled in with his travel trailer and was setting up camp a few sites over. His voice, however, had that tone I've come to recognize after years of RVing: the "I've got a problem and I don't know what to do" tone.

* * *

"Hey, Stan, you got a minute? I can't get water to my sink or shower."

So, book down, hat on, and over I went. Sure enough, on the back of his trailer there were two hose connections. One was clearly labeled *City Water Connection*. The other? No label. Just a lonely brass fitting daring someone to guess what it might be for.

I didn't like the feeling creeping into my gut.

I checked his setup. The hose was connected... but not to the city water inlet. No, sir. He had hooked up to the *black tank flush*. Now, for those who might not be familiar, the black tank flush is designed to spray water inside your sewage tank to rinse it out—*after* you've dumped it. If you leave the valve closed and pump water in, it's basically the RV equivalent of filling a water balloon until it bursts.

I asked him if he'd noticed water running anywhere strange. He pointed to the roof. "Yeah, I thought maybe the air conditioner was leaking."

Oh, it was leaking all right. Just not what he thought.

See, when your black tank is so full it's got nowhere else to go, it finds a way. In this case, it was burping up and out of the roof vent. The sight of brown water streaking off a white travel trailer is one of those images you never forget.

Still trying to give him the benefit of the doubt, I asked, "No water coming out of the sinks? The shower?"

He shook his head.

And that's when my stomach sank. I knew exactly what had happened. He had overfilled his black tank to the point of eruption.

We quickly moved the hose to the correct connection, and—like magic—his faucets sprang to life. He grinned, relieved. Me? I wasn't grinning. I had that uneasy, twitchy feeling you get when you know the worst is still waiting around the corner.

* * *

I excused myself, walked into his bathroom, and pressed the flush pedal on the toilet.

And that's when it happened.

Mount Vesuvius erupted.

Not steam, not lava—something far worse. With a violent gurgle, his black tank unleashed its fury straight upward, and I happened to be standing in ground zero. One second I was pressing a pedal, the next I was baptized in a shower of sewage.

I don't remember exactly what words came out of my mouth, but I can promise you they were not the kind you repeat in Sunday school. Somewhere in the chaos I yelled, slammed the toilet lid down, and stumbled backward like I'd just survived a geyser in Yellowstone.

The smell? Let's not dwell on that. Let's just say it was memorable.

By the time the eruption subsided, I was standing there dripping, shoes ruined, dignity long gone. And then—I laughed. I couldn't help it. Because honestly, what else do you do when you've just taken your third shower of the day: one planned, one courtesy of a toilet, and one to wash the aftermath off yourself?

Meanwhile, my friend stood there wide-eyed, like a kid who just set off fireworks in the living room. "I'm so sorry," he stammered.

I waved him off. "Buddy, don't apologize. Just learn. And maybe buy me a new shirt."

Here's the thing: he wasn't a rookie. He's been RVing for years. But that's the Black Tank Blues for you—they don't care if it's your first trip or your hundredth. One wrong connection, one overlooked label, and suddenly you've created a story that will follow you forever.

My recommendation, which I now share with anyone who will listen, is simple: **pay attention to your connections.** Labels exist for a reason. If your rig doesn't have labels, get a Sharpie, a label maker, or carve one out of wood if you have to. Because the last thing you want is to confuse your city water inlet with your black tank flush. Trust me, it's a mistake you only make once.

As for me, I went back to Bertie Bea, peeled off my foul-smelling clothes, and took another long, scalding shower. I poured myself a stiff drink, sat back under the awning, and shook my head. The Black Tank Blues had struck again—only this time, I wasn't even the one at fault.

But that's the way RV life goes. Sometimes you're the victim of your own mistakes, and sometimes you're just standing in the wrong place at the wrong time. Either way, you learn, you laugh, and eventually you tell the story.

And if you're me, you also buy bulk soap, because you never know when you'll need your third shower of the day.

CHAPTER THREE

Drenched in Dodge City and other Storm Stories

One of the biggest myths about RV life is that it's all sunsets, sunrises, and perfectly staged Instagram photos. You know the ones—an RV parked just so, golden light spilling over the mountains, camp chairs set up with steaming mugs of coffee that never get cold. Don't get me wrong, I've seen my fair share of breathtaking sunsets and awe-inspiring mornings on the road, and I wouldn't trade them for anything. But those picture-perfect moments don't come without their opposite: storms. Big ones. The kind of storms that leave you wondering why in the world you thought rolling your house on wheels across the country was a good idea.

Weather has a way of humbling you, especially when you live in an RV. At home, bad weather might mean you turn up the thermostat or retreat to the basement with some candles. On the road, though? Bad weather means you're parked in a 20,000-pound box that may or may not act like a kite if the wind gusts just right. Add in slides, awnings, and roof vents, and suddenly Mother Nature feels less like a mild inconvenience and more like a high-stakes chess game where she's always three moves ahead.

Over the past five years, I've had my share of encounters with thunderstorms, hailstorms, and wind events that tested both my patience and Bertie Bea's durability. Some of these stories still make me shake my head. Others I can laugh at now—though at the time, I was too busy praying that my slides would retract, my roof would hold, and my awning wouldn't end up in the neighbor's campsite like some kind of twisted offering.

* * *

Take awnings, for instance. They're like the toddler of RV accessories: charming, useful, but impossible to trust when you turn your back. I've seen more shredded awnings in campgrounds than I can count, and they all have the same origin story. Someone thought, "The weather looks fine, no need to bring it in." Then, around two in the morning, the wind picks up, a thunderstorm rolls through, and suddenly that handy shade cover has transformed into a mangled mess of fabric and metal flapping against the side of the rig. That's why I bring my awning in every single evening, no matter how calm or clear the skies look. I'd rather sip coffee in the morning without shade than sip it while mourning the $1,200 I just lost to Mother Nature.

Slides are another story altogether. They're great when they work—your living room expands, your bedroom feels bigger, and you get to brag about all the "extra space." But slides are also magnets for trouble when storms roll through. Heavy rain can find its way into seals, a stiff wind can rock them just enough to cause mechanical strain, and hail? Well, let's just say that's not a sound anyone wants to hear pounding on the side of their slide topper at three a.m.

One storm in particular stands out to me—the morning I got drenched in Dodge City. What should have been a simple stop turned into one of those nights where everything that could go wrong did go wrong. A stubborn slide that refused to retract, rain coming down sideways, lightning lighting up the prairie like a strobe light—it was the kind of scene that makes you second-guess whether RV life is for you. Spoiler alert: it is, but only if you're willing to laugh about it later.

That's the thing about weather on the road. It's not something to fear, but it is something you'd better respect. Ignoring it, underestimating it, or thinking you can outsmart it usually ends up with very expensive lessons. Mother Nature doesn't care that you had dinner plans or that you wanted to sleep in. She'll send a wind gust that knocks your satellite dish off, or drop hailstones the size of marbles just to remind you who's in charge.

So, you learn. You learn to check the radar even when the sky looks clear. You learn to pull the awning in before bed. You learn that sometimes the smartest thing you can do is button up, pull the slides in, and wait it out. And yes, you learn to keep extra towels handy, because sooner or later, you'll end up drenched.

In this chapter, I'm going to share a few of those stories—the storms that turned ordinary evenings into unforgettable adventures. Stories of wind, rain, and the occasional hailstone that tested my patience, my equipment, and sometimes my sense of humor. They weren't fun at the time, but now? They've become part of the collection of tales I carry with me, reminders that the road isn't always smooth, but it's always worth it.

Because in the end, storms are just part of the deal. They come and they go, sometimes with fury, sometimes with a light show you'll never forget. And if you're lucky—and prepared—you'll come out the other side with your rig intact, your sense of humor stronger, and maybe even a story worth telling.

Dodge City Slide Issues in Thunderstorm

On Sunday morning, June 30, 2024, I woke up in the Gunsmoke RV Park in Dodge City, Kansas. Fitting name, because by the end of the day, I was ready to duel it out with Bertie Bea's slide system at high noon. It was a travel day, and the plan was simple: roll out, hook up Rosie, and make the 180-mile drive to the Wellington KOA Holiday for a quick overnight. But as every RVer knows, Mother Nature and Murphy's Law sometimes travel together.

Right about the time I was packing up, Mother Nature decided it was the perfect moment for one of those classic high plains thunderstorms.

You know the kind—sky so dark it feels like midnight, thunder rumbling like cannon fire, and rain that comes at you sideways. The timing couldn't have been worse. I had my pre-trip checklist going, Bertie Bea's engine running, and I was at the point where all that was left was pulling in the slides.

The vanity slide slid in without complaint. Smooth, easy, like a well-trained dog coming when it's called. The bedroom slide, though? Nothing. I pressed the button. Waited. Pressed it again. Still nothing. That slide sat there stubbornly like a mule that had dug in its heels and said, "Nope, not today, pal."

Now, this was new. I'd never had a slide refuse to budge before, and my frustration level skyrocketed in about three seconds. For five long minutes, I stood there, pressing the button over and over, as if—just maybe—the definition of insanity wouldn't apply to me this time. Spoiler alert: it did.

So, I did what every responsible RVer eventually does: I reached for the manuals. Out came the thick binder of Bertie Bea's collected wisdom. Somewhere in that stack of technical jargon and diagrams was the answer to my problem. Sure enough, I found the instructions for the Lippert Schwintek slide system. Turns out, there's a reset process for the controller. Great! Problem solved! Except... I had no idea where the controller was.

A little hunting around, and I realized it was tucked away in the passenger-side rear bay. Outside. In the thunderstorm. Of course.

So, I put on my raincoat, grabbed my trusty pointy needle-nose pliers (the RV tool you never knew you'd need until you desperately need it), and stepped out into the downpour. The rain pelted me so hard I felt like I'd walked into a car wash. Thunder cracked overhead as I crouched down at the bay, fumbling with wet fingers to press the little reset button six times and then hold it on the seventh until both the red and green lights flashed.

It worked. I trudged back inside, dripping like a Labrador fresh out of a lake, and hit the button again. This time, the bedroom slide retracted. Victory! Or at least a partial victory. Because by now, I was soaked to the bone.

I finished my pre-trip checklist as fast as I could, but in my haste, I left my trusty step stool and door mat sitting outside. Somewhere out there, in Dodge City, is a very confused camper wondering why someone abandoned perfectly good RV gear.

Before I could pull out of the site, I had to duck into the tiny bathroom —slides in, mind you—and change clothes. If you've never tried to change out of soaking wet jeans in an RV bathroom the size of a broom closet, let me tell you: it's less like changing clothes and more like competitive yoga.

Finally, Rosie was hooked up, plugged in, and ready to roll. The drive to Wellington, Kansas, was 180 miles of pure torture. Standing water covered the roads, wipers struggled to keep up, and I white-knuckled the steering wheel the whole way. Then, like some cosmic joke, the minute I hit Interstate 35 South, the skies cleared. Sunlight poured down, the pavement dried up, and the last stretch into the KOA was perfectly uneventful.

But Dodge City wasn't quite finished teaching me a lesson. For the rest of that trip, every single morning, I had to reset the Lippert controller to get that stubborn slide to move. By the time I made it to Red Bay and the Bob Tiffin Service Center, I learned the real culprit: a worn cable. Every time the slide went all the way out, it rubbed against the wiring just enough to cause a short. When the slide was in, it behaved fine. Out? Total mutiny.

The fix was simple: replace the cable. But the experience was anything but simple. It was wet, messy, frustrating, and humbling. And like most of my RV misadventures, it came with a side order of humor— though it took me a while to laugh about it.

Lesson learned? Storms happen. Slides fail. And sometimes, you end up standing in the rain with a pair of pliers, praying for flashing lights like you're playing some twisted arcade game. But you get through it, you dry off, and you keep rolling. Because in the end, that's what RV life is all about.

Kit Carson and the High Plains Winds

In May 2025, I decided to visit Kit Carson, Colorado, for a week. Now, when you hear the name Kit Carson, you picture rugged mountain men, frontier history, and maybe even a museum dedicated to the legendary explorer himself. What you don't picture—or at least what *I* didn't picture—is a town so small and remote that the nearest grocery store is a Dollar General 25 miles away.

That was lesson number one. When you plan a weeklong stop in the middle of nowhere Colorado, make sure you've stocked up on supplies. Otherwise, your options boil down to driving half an hour for canned ravioli or surviving on whatever snacks you can find in Rosie's glove box. But hey, they did have a Kit Carson museum, which gave me at least one thing to brag about when people asked why in the world I picked Kit Carson for a destination.

The first few days went fine. Quiet campground, big skies, and that sense of peace you only find on the high plains where you can watch your dog run away for three days. And then came Wednesday, May 14. That's when I got my next lesson: never underestimate the wind on the Colorado plains.

It started as a breeze. By late morning it had turned into a stiff wind. By afternoon, it was a full-on event. Sustained winds at 35 miles per hour, gusts up to 70. Seventy miles per hour! That's not a breeze, that's Mother Nature testing her new leaf blower.

Now, RVers know that wind is nothing to mess around with. A little rocking here and there, no problem. But once the gusts get up into the

50s and beyond, things start moving that aren't supposed to move. In my case, the slide toppers—those fabric awnings that cover the tops of the slides—started flapping like they were trying to rip themselves free. I swear I could hear them begging for mercy. Every time a gust hit, the rollers would snap and groan, and I imagined the fabric flying off into Kansas like a wayward kite.

After about an hour of listening to that constant flapping, I made the call. Comfort was one thing, safety was another. It was time to bring in all four of Bertie Bea's slides and hunker down. When the slides are in, Bertie is more compact, less of a broadside target for the wind, and the slide toppers get a break from their punishment.

The process was quick, though not without its own brand of inconvenience. With all the slides in, Bertie Bea turns into something that feels less like a rolling home and more like a rolling studio apartment in Manhattan. My king-sized bed? Suddenly shortened, with about six inches of it tucked under the closet on the vanity slide side. My living room? Gone, swallowed up as the walls crept inward. My kitchen? Let's just say you learn to appreciate counter space when you lose it.

Sleeping that night felt a little like bunking in a shoebox. I stretched out on the bed, feet brushing against the closet, ceiling creaking as the wind battered us outside. Every gust shook Bertie Bea just enough to remind me that we were guests in the middle of the high plains, and Mother Nature was the landlord.

But here's the thing: I slept better than I thought I would. Not because it was comfortable—it wasn't—but because I knew Bertie Bea was in her safest configuration. The slides were in, the toppers weren't flapping themselves into oblivion, and we presented a much smaller profile to the relentless wind. Safety trumped comfort, and that's a trade I'll make every time.

When morning came, the winds had died down, the sun was shining, and Bertie Bea was still standing strong. My step stool hadn't blown into Nebraska, my awning hadn't shredded itself to pieces, and the slide toppers were still intact. I stepped outside, took a deep breath of that crisp Colorado air, and thought, "Well, that wasn't so bad."

* * *

Of course, it *was* bad in the moment—loud, cramped, and nerve-wracking—but like so many RV adventures, the discomfort fades while the story sticks around. And this one came with a clear takeaway:

When you're parked out on the high plains, comfort is optional. Safety isn't.

So, if you ever find yourself in Kit Carson—or anywhere with wide-open spaces and nothing to slow the wind—don't ignore the forecast. Don't assume your slide toppers can take it. And definitely don't convince yourself that "just one more night with the slides out" will be fine. It won't.

The high plains will remind you who's in charge, and all you can do is respect that, pull everything in, and wait it out.

At the end of the day, I came to Kit Carson for a little history and a quiet week, but I left with a new appreciation for wind, a tighter relationship with my RV, and a story worth telling. Not bad for a town with a Dollar General 25 miles down the road.

CHAPTER FOUR
Awning Meets Its Match

If there's one thing I've learned in five years on the road, it's this: the pre-trip checklist is not just a suggestion. It's not a "maybe I'll do it today" kind of thing. It's not even a "close enough" kind of thing. It is a sacred ritual. A requirement. A survival tool that separates those who roll smoothly down the highway from those who find themselves standing in a campground driveway, staring at a mangled awning arm and muttering words unfit for polite company.

Now, I'd love to sit here and tell you that I've always been disciplined about following that checklist. That I approach it with the same devotion a pilot gives to their pre-flight walkaround. That I never cut corners, never forget a step, never let my excitement to hit the road override my better judgment. I'd love to tell you that—but it would be a lie.

The truth is, I've skipped a step or two. Or three. And let me tell you, every single time I've treated that checklist like a "loose set of guidelines" instead of the gospel, it has come back to bite me. Hard.

That's the thing about RVing—every mistake has consequences. Forget to latch a cabinet? You'll be picking up canned soup off the floor at the next stoplight. Forget to bring in your steps? They'll drag down the road like a very expensive curb feeler. And forget to bring in your awning? Well, let's just say that's how this chapter got its name: *Awning Meets Its Match*.

See, the checklist is there to protect you from yourself. It's easy to underestimate just how many moving parts an RV has. It's not like hopping into a car where you check your mirrors, buckle your seatbelt, and drive away. No, an RV is a rolling house with slides, jacks, awnings, antennas, vents, hookups, and about fifty other things that can turn into expensive disasters if you leave them in the wrong position.

I can't tell you how many times I've been packing up in a campground, chatting with neighbors, trying to beat the check-out time, or just plain eager to get rolling, when I've been tempted to rush. "It's fine," I'll tell myself. "I know the steps by heart. I don't need the checklist this time."

That is exactly the moment when the RV gods sit back, smile, and say, "Oh, really? Let's see how that works out for you."

And they never fail to deliver a reminder.

One of my personal greatest hits was the time I forgot to retract Bessie's awning before leaving the Alsatian RV Resort in Texas. Yep, you read that right. I pulled out of a perfectly nice RV park, waving at the staff like everything was normal, while my awning stretched proudly out like a flag announcing to the world, *"This guy forgot his checklist."* It wasn't until the awning arm met the unforgiving resistance of a gatepost that I realized my mistake. Metal bent, fabric tore, and my pride took the biggest hit of all.

Now, was it funny in the moment? Absolutely not. Did I laugh later? Oh, you bet. Because when you're standing there trying to explain to yourself how you could forget something as obvious as a 16-foot awning sticking out the side of your motorhome, there's nothing left to do but laugh. And maybe add a new line to the checklist written in all caps: **AWNING IN.**

That's the thing about mistakes on the road: they hurt in the moment, but they make for the best stories later. And they reinforce why the checklist is non-negotiable.

Over the years, I've developed my own system to make sure I don't repeat the same boneheaded moves. I walk around Bertie Bea before every departure, double-check the slides, the jacks, the hookups, the steps, and yes, the awning. I do it rain or shine, tired or wide awake, because I know that one skipped step can turn a smooth travel day into an expensive lesson.

But even with all that experience, I'll admit—I'm still human. Distractions happen. Mistakes happen. And sometimes, the only way you learn is by replacing an awning, buying a new step stool, or fishing your doormat out of a campground dumpster.

In this chapter, I will share some of those stories. Stories from the times I treated my checklist like an optional suggestion instead of the ironclad rule it is. Stories where rushing, distraction, or just plain stubbornness led to "interesting" results. Painful at the time, hilarious later.

Ultimately, the checklist isn't there to ruin your fun or slow you down. It's there to save you from yourself. And trust me, as someone who's learned the hard way, you *will* forget something eventually. The only question is whether you'll catch it before your awning meets its match.

Awning Meets Its Match: The Alsatian Incident

In December 2020, Bessie (my 2013 Forest River Sunseeker 2300) and I rolled down to Castroville, Texas, with Rosie faithfully in tow. We were fresh off a trip to Fort Worth, where I'd gone to see the National Finals Rodeo. Normally the NFR takes place in Las Vegas, but thanks to COVID restrictions, it had been relocated to Texas. Cowboys, broncs, and bulls—it felt good to get a dose of rodeo life, even if the setting was different.

After the rodeo, I decided to tack on a week at the Alsatian RV Resort in Castroville. The place had come highly recommended by several of the YouTube influencers I'd been binge-watching at the time. Back then, I was still new to RV life, soaking up every tip and trick I could find on YouTube, Instagram, or from fellow RVers in campgrounds. If someone with a drone and a cowboy hat said, "This is the best resort in Texas," I was inclined to believe them.

Alsatian did not disappoint. The grounds were immaculate, the sites were spacious, and the vibe was friendly. Castroville itself had a small-town charm, and San Antonio was only a short drive away. That week, I visited friends in the city, stood at the Alamo, and tried to imagine what it must've been like in 1836 when Santa Anna and the Mexican Army overran it. I got to blend my love of history with my new RV lifestyle, and for the most part, the week was uneventful in the best way.

Until Saturday, December 12.

The weather had been gorgeous all week—sunny and warm—so I had

Bessie's awning out nearly the whole time. No problem there. But here's the catch: Bessie didn't have slides, and she didn't have any of those fancy built-in safety interlocks that keep you from driving away if something is still deployed. She was old-school. If you forgot to bring something in, well, that was on you.

Guess who forgot to bring something in?

Yep. When it came time to pack up and leave, I went through my pre-trip checklist—or at least I thought I did. In my mind, I had everything covered. Water disconnected, sewer dumped, electric unplugged, leveling blocks stored, Rosie hooked up—check, check, check. I was feeling confident, like I'd finally hit my stride as an RVer.

What didn't I check? The awning.

So there we were, Bessie chugging along, Rosie obediently following behind, as I rolled toward the exit gate. The awning was still out, flapping proudly like a victory banner announcing to the world: *"Here goes a guy who thinks he's got it all figured out!"*

Now, in my defense, I think a few kind souls in the campground *tried* to wave me down. I remember seeing people gesturing and pointing, but I just thought, "Well, folks around here sure are friendly." Nope. They weren't waving hello—they were trying to save me from myself.

By the time I realized what was happening, it was too late. The awning arm met the gatepost with all the grace of a linebacker hitting a tackling dummy. Thankfully, the resort had installed a breakaway piece on the gatepost—probably because they'd seen more than one rookie make the same mistake. The post gave way with a loud crack, saving my awning from total destruction. Minimal damage to the awning, minimal damage to the gate, but maximum damage to my pride.

I sat there for a second, stunned. One part of me wanted to crawl under the driver's seat and hide. The other part wanted to throw the checklist out the window and yell, "What's the point if I'm just going to forget the obvious stuff anyway?"

* * *

Instead, I climbed out, surveyed the scene, and did the only thing I could do: laugh. A sheepish, nervous laugh, the kind you let out when you know you've just broadcast your rookie status to the entire campground.

The damage wasn't bad. A little bend in the awning arm, a little scuff on the fabric, and a bruised ego that would take longer to heal. But it could have been much worse. Had there not been that breakaway piece on the gate, I might have ripped the awning clean off. That would've been an expensive repair—and possibly the end of my trip.

And that's the funny thing. At the time, it felt like a disaster. But looking back, I realize that incident could've derailed my pursuit of this lifestyle entirely. A big, costly repair on my first rig, during my first year, might've made me give up and say, "You know what? Maybe the RV life isn't for me."

Instead, it was simply a lesson. An embarrassing, loud, somewhat destructive lesson—but a lesson nonetheless. Always, always stick to the checklist. Especially the part about the awning.

The rest of my trip went fine. I drove back east to Kick Back Ranch in Alabama, then on to North Carolina for Christmas with family. Bessie, bruised but not broken, carried me the whole way without complaint. Rosie didn't mind either—she was probably just grateful not to have been dragged into the mess.

Looking back now, that Alsatian incident is one of those stories I tell with a smile. It wasn't funny then, but it's hilarious now. And every time I roll up the awning before pulling out of a site, I think of that gatepost in Castroville and whisper, "Not today."

Because in this lifestyle, you can either let your mistakes defeat you, or you can laugh, learn, and keep rolling. I chose to laugh.

The Checklist Chronicles: Ruston, Facebook, and a Slide Full of Rain

Friday, May 2, 2025, started like many of my travel days do: Bertie Bea fired up, Rosie dutifully in tow, and me rolling out of Kick Back Ranch & Event Center in Ramer, Alabama—my "home base" when I'm not on the road. Kick Back isn't just a place to park; it's a second home, the kind of campground where folks know your name, wave when you pull in, and sometimes offer unsolicited advice on how to back into your site (whether you need it or not).

This trip was different, though. It was bittersweet. I was headed to Dallas for my *last* week of employment with a large telecom company. After years of punching the clock, juggling meetings, and managing projects, I was finally on the edge of something new—trading in the corporate grind for the open road full-time. But first, I had to make it through one last week of in-office work.

That Friday night, I pulled into the Meridian East/Toomsuba KOA Journey in Toomsuba, Mississippi. It's not the Ritz, but it's a solid overnight stop, easy in and out, and close enough to the interstate to make the next day's drive simple. I leveled Bertie Bea, put out the slides, hooked up the utilities, and settled in for the evening.

About an hour later, the skies opened up. One of those classic late-spring thunderstorms—the kind that turns ditches into rivers and makes you wonder if you should start gathering animals two by two. I'm not exaggerating when I say two to three inches of rain fell in a very short time. It hammered the roof, pooled in the grass, and collected on top of the slide toppers like they were inflatable kiddie pools.

I wasn't too worried. Slide toppers are designed for this kind of thing. They take the brunt of the rain, leaves, and debris so your slides don't. But I also knew there'd be a lot of water waiting for me in the morning.

The next day, Saturday, I packed up to head toward Piney Hills RV Park in Ruston, Louisiana. As always, I pulled out my trusty pre-trip checklist. I've learned the hard way—multiple times—that skipping the checklist is like playing Russian roulette with your rig. Forget one thing and you'll pay for it later. So I went down the list carefully, step by step. Or at least I thought I did.

Slides in? Check. Jacks up? Check. Utilities disconnected? Check. Steps up? Check. Rosie hooked up? Check. Awning in? Double-check. Everything looked good. I hit the road feeling like a responsible, seasoned RVer who had learned from his mistakes.

But RV life has a funny way of humbling you at the exact moment you think you've got it all figured out.

Somewhere along I-20, I stopped for gas. That's when I noticed something odd on the driver's side. The metal cover on top of the slide topper looked… wrong. Not catastrophic, but not right either. It was wedged between the slide rail and the side of Bertie Bea like it had tried to escape and gotten caught in the act.

* * *

My heart sank. *What did I do this time?*

It didn't take long to figure it out. When I pulled in the slide that morning, all that pooled water from the thunderstorm the night before came rushing off. But instead of waiting a few extra minutes for it to finish draining before retracting the slide, I rushed it. That flood of water pushed the metal cover just enough to get it stuck.

Cue the frustration. Here I was, at a truck stop in Mississippi, staring at a bent-looking slide cover, wondering if I had just bought myself a costly lesson in patience.

Now, usually my rule is simple: troubleshoot first, *then* phone a friend. But in that moment, I broke my own rule. I snapped a picture and posted it on Facebook. Within minutes, my phone lit up like a Christmas tree. Comments poured in. Everyone had advice, theories, and horror stories to share. Some said it looked fine, others swore it was ruined, and one person suggested duct tape (there's always one).

Meanwhile, I still hadn't actually tried anything. Finally, common sense kicked back in. I cranked up the generator, walked over to the slide controls, and extended the slide out again. Then I waited. Two minutes. Three minutes. Long enough to make sure every drop of water had drained.

Then I hit the retract button. Smooth as butter. The cover slid back into place like nothing had ever happened. Crisis averted.

I stood there shaking my head. Hours of worry, a Facebook thread a mile long, and the whole thing came down to me not giving gravity enough time to do its job. All I had needed was patience. And a reminder that Facebook is better for sharing pictures of sunsets than diagnosing RV issues.

From that day on, I added a new step to my mental checklist: after pulling in the slides, do a walkaround. Every time. Rain or shine. Because it's one thing to think you've checked everything, and another to actually lay eyes on it.

The main point? Even when you're careful, it's the small details that cause problems. A few gallons of rainwater, a few seconds of rushing, and suddenly you're in a truck stop parking lot wondering if you've damaged your rig.

RV life has a way of keeping you humble, but it also teaches you lessons you won't forget. That day, I learned patience, the importance of a walkaround, and that Facebook isn't always the best troubleshooting tool.

And if I'm being honest, I also learned that a bit of humor goes a long way. Because once the panic subsided, I had to laugh. There I was, worried sick about a bent slide topper, when all it took to fix it was the same thing it takes to cook pasta: give it time.

CHAPTER FIVE

Parking on a Postage Stamp and Other Tight Spots

One of the first things you realize when you graduate from a Class C to a Class A motorhome is this: you're no longer driving something that fits *anywhere*. You're driving a small apartment strapped to a bus chassis. Add in a tow bar and a car on the back, and suddenly you're 55 feet long and moving through the world like an 18-wheeler without the luxury of a CDL.

For me, that small apartment is Bertie Bea, my 36-foot Tiffin Allegro Open Road 34PA. And faithfully tagging along behind her is Rosie, my Chevy Equinox tow car. Together, we're a respectable 55 feet long. Which sounds fine until you actually try to wedge all of that into the average gas station or an undersized RV site that looks like it was designed back when the biggest rigs on the road were pop-ups and pickup campers.

When I first hit the road, I assumed campgrounds were built with big rigs in mind. After all, RVs have gotten bigger over the years. Surely, most parks had adapted. Wrong. While plenty of places do have nice pull-through sites that can accommodate Bertie Bea and Rosie without complaint, there are still plenty of campgrounds—and gas stations—that make me wonder if I should just carry a can of spray paint to mark my own "extended" parking lines.

Whenever possible, I try to book pull-through sites. They're the holy grail for us, longer rigs. Drive in, hook up, relax, and when it's time to leave, you roll right out again. No complicated backing maneuvers, no ten-point turns while your neighbors set up lawn chairs to watch the show, no unhooking Rosie to squeeze in. Pull-through sites are sanity savers.

But life on the road isn't always that smooth. Over the past couple of years with Bertie Bea, I can count about ten times when I pulled into a campground, looked at my assigned site, and thought, *There is no way this is going to work.* It's that sinking feeling when you stare down a site that looks more suited for a teardrop trailer than a Class A motorhome. Sometimes I wonder if campgrounds hand out sites as part of a practical joke.

And then there's fueling up. If campgrounds are the test of your patience, gas stations are the test of your courage. Every time I roll into one, I break into a light sweat. I'm scanning the lot like I'm playing a real-life version of Tetris, looking for the one pump at the end that points back out to the road. That's the only pump I can use without risking a nightmare scenario: having to back up with Rosie still attached.

See, here's the thing four-wheeler drivers don't understand: when you're 55 feet long and flat-towing a car, you don't *back up*. At least, not without breaking something expensive. The tow bar isn't designed for reverse. You want to back up? Fine, but you'll be dragging Rosie sideways, shredding her tires, bending metal, and possibly explaining to your insurance company why your tow car now looks like a crushed soda can. That means every gas station has to be carefully chosen and executed.

But try explaining that to the guy in the pickup who thinks I'm just being picky when I insist on waiting for the end pump to clear. No, friend, I'm not being fussy. I'm trying to avoid turning my road trip into a costly lesson in geometry.

Between fueling up and campsite roulette, these are easily two of the most stressful parts of RV life. Forget driving through the mountains in a crosswind, or threading your way through downtown traffic with low bridges and tight turns—those things I can handle. But put me in a cramped gas station with a line of cars honking behind me? Or a campsite so tight I wonder if the park ranger is secretly running a reality TV show? That's when my blood pressure really spikes.

* * *

The problem with both situations is the same: there's no room for error. A mistake in a wide-open field might mean you dent your pride. A mistake in a cramped gas station or campsite can result in bent sheet metal, busted fiberglass, or worse. Repairs don't come cheap in the RV world, and you can bet they never happen at a convenient time.

That's why I take these situations seriously. They may sound funny—and trust me, they often are funny afterward—but in the moment, there's a lot riding on it. And still, despite the stress, they always end up giving me a story worth sharing.

In this chapter, I will share two of those stories. The first takes us all the way to Washington State, where I tried to park at a friend's house and discovered that "plenty of room" means very different things to people who don't drive motorhomes. The second takes us to a KOA in Montana, where I was pretty sure I'd need a shoehorn to fit Bertie Bea and Rosie into the space they called a "site."

Both stories highlight the reality of RV life: sometimes you're gliding into a spacious pull-through like a pro, and sometimes you're sweating bullets trying not to take out a tree, a power pedestal, or your own mirror. Either way, you learn to laugh about it later. Because if you don't, well, you might as well trade in the motorhome for a tent.

Parking on a Postage Stamp: The Loon Lake Shuffle

The Summer RV Tour of 2023 will always hold a special place in my memory. It was the first big adventure in Bertie Bea with Rosie faithfully in tow, and with that came a steep learning curve. One of the biggest lessons from that trip? Knowing just how much real estate a 36-foot motorhome plus 20 feet of tow bar and tow car really needs to operate without drama. Spoiler alert: a lot more than I had that day at Loon Lake, Washington.

It was late June when I rolled into the area, headed to a friend's house for a few days by the water. I'd been looking forward to this stop for months—time with old friends, lake views, and the kind of relaxation you only get when you can sit outside with a cup of coffee and listen to loons call across the water. Sounds idyllic, right?

And it would have been, if not for the driveway.

When I arrived and saw the space I was supposed to fit Bertie Bea into, I felt my stomach drop. The driveway was brand-new asphalt, a glossy 12 feet wide, lined tightly on one side with trees. On the other side sat their garage outbuilding, standing guard like it was daring me to come too close. Once I got Bertie Bea parked with all four slides out, I calculated I'd have about one foot of breathing room between her wall and the building. That's not a parking spot—that's threading a needle.

Oh, and to spice things up, their septic tank sat about five feet beyond the edge of the driveway. Which meant the margin of error was basically zero. On one side: building scrapes and fiberglass repairs. On the other: "Congratulations, you've just driven over the septic tank."

***

Parking Bertie Bea suddenly felt like trying to land a 747 on a high school football field.

The whole setup didn't help either. Their home was tucked into a wooded corner that doubled as a kids' summer camp. That meant the access roads were narrow, with low-hanging branches that seemed just a little too interested in Bertie's rooftop air conditioners. I had visions of driving out with one AC unit shaved clean off, dangling like a trophy from a cottonwood.

I knew immediately that Rosie had to come off the tow bar. She'd only get in the way during what was shaping up to be an Olympic-level parking event. I unhooked her, pulled her aside, and braced myself.

Here's the thing about tight spaces in an RV: you can't just whip in like you're parallel parking a sedan. Every move has to be deliberate. You turn the wheel six inches too far, and suddenly you're trimming trees, denting sheet metal, or worse. The key is patience. Slow, steady, and—most importantly—getting out to look. Over and over and over again.

And that's precisely what I did. I inched forward, cranked the wheel, backed up, straightened out, and repeated the process. Again. And again. And again. If you'd watched the footage from my dashcam, you'd swear I was playing a giant game of Tetris, trying to fit Bertie Bea into a space clearly designed for something half her size.

By the time I finally had her snugged up against the garage, I'd done roughly a 100-point turn. Not a 3-point turn. Not even a 20-point turn. A full 100-point turn, complete with muttered curses, a few words that would've made a sailor blush, and enough back-and-forth movement to make the neighbors wonder if I was training for a NASCAR pit crew.

***

But you know what? I made it.

Bertie Bea was tucked in, with her slides extended, offering about a foot of clearance on one side next to the building and a beautiful view of the lake and the house on the other. No damage, and the septic tank was still intact. I stepped back, sweaty and exhausted, and let out the kind of relieved laugh you only get when you've pulled off the seemingly impossible.

* * *

The real kicker? The whole ordeal was captured on my dashcam. Every grunt, every stop, every gear shift is preserved forever on video. I haven't decided if I'll ever share it publicly—there's only so much humiliation a man can take—but I will say this: it's comedy gold.

Of course, getting in is only half the battle. Getting out is where things really get interesting.

* * *

When it came time to leave, I quickly realized there was no way I could pull forward and swing Bertie Bea around. The driveway didn't have the space. The only option was to back her all the way out. And if you've never backed a Class A motorhome down a narrow driveway lined with trees, let me tell you—it's a character-building experience.

Once again, Rosie had to sit out. I left her unhooked until I was free and clear of the squeeze. Mirrors adjusted, hazards on, I slowly inched Bertie Bea backward, praying the whole time that no curious camper kids wandered into my blind spots. My heart rate was somewhere north of "first date nerves" and edging into "job interview with the CEO" territory.

But eventually, I emerged victorious. Bertie Bea eased onto the road without a scratch, without a bent mirror, and with all rooftop equipment still intact. Rosie got hooked back up, and off we went to the next adventure.

The rest of the Loon Lake visit was bliss. Time with friends, evenings by the water, laughter, and the kind of conversations that make road trips worth it. But that parking job? That's the part I'll never forget.

The takeaway was simple: just because someone says they have "plenty of room" for your RV doesn't mean they actually do. Non-RVers think in terms of driveways and minivans. RVers think in terms of clearance angles, slide extensions, and septic tanks waiting like land mines. Those two languages don't always translate.

And if you ever find yourself in a spot like that, remember this: go slow. Get out and look. Then get out and look again. Repeat as many times as necessary. Because patience is the only way you'll ever park a rig the size of Bertie Bea on a space the size of a postage stamp.

Was it stressful? Absolutely. Would I do it again? Sure—though maybe next time I'll insist we meet at a campground with pull-throughs. But here's the truth: it's moments like these that make RV life what it is. You can plan all you want, you can follow your checklist religiously, but sooner or later, you'll find yourself in a driveway in Washington State, sweating bullets, wondering how on earth you're going to pull this off.

And then, somehow, you do.

Big Timber, Big Trouble

By the time you've driven a rig the size of Bertie Bea long enough, you start to assume that when you book a pull-through site, you're getting something reasonably sized. It's the RV equivalent of ordering a burger at a diner—you just expect it to come with meat, a bun, and maybe a pickle. But every so often, you order the "burger" and what arrives is closer to a slider with a side of disappointment.

That was the case with the Big Timber/Greycliff KOA Journey in Montana during my Summer RV Tour of 2023.

I was on my way to Washington State, and after leaving Cody, Wyoming, I figured Big Timber would make a nice overnight stop. I booked a pull-through site in advance because, well, 36 feet of Bertie Bea plus 20 feet of tow bar and Rosie isn't something you just wedge into a random space. Pull-throughs make life easier. No unhooking, no gymnastics, no stress. At least that's the theory.

The arrival started fine. I checked in at the office, smiled politely, and followed the campground host's golf cart toward my assigned site. That's when things started to unravel.

The road to the site looked less like a road and more like a deer trail—narrow, muddy, and with ruts that made me wonder if maybe this was part of the Lewis and Clark Trail nobody had paved yet. Just across from my site was a little stream, which might sound quaint if you're picturing it in a postcard. But when you're driving 24,500 pounds of motorhome, a stream is less "quaint" and more "hazard." Add in a tree strategically placed right where I'd need to turn out to the right, and suddenly this "pull-through" was starting to look more like a practical joke.

And then I actually saw the site.

I've seen parking spots at Walmart bigger than this so-called pull-through. It was so short that only Bertie Bea could fit. Rosie, faithful and patient as ever, had to be parked in front of her like an accessory someone bolted on as an afterthought. I sat there behind the wheel, looking at the space, and thought, *This can't be right*. But the host in the golf cart just waved cheerfully and sped off, leaving me to figure it out.

So, I squeezed Bertie Bea into the space, tucked Rosie in front, and made the best of it. Once we were parked, the night was uneventful enough. I hooked up, leveled, and tried to ignore the tree that loomed over my exit path like a bouncer deciding whether or not I'd be allowed to leave in the morning.

When morning came, I did what any self-respecting RVer does: I sized up the situation with a cup of coffee in hand and tried to figure out the least disastrous way out. The official way to leave was to pull forward, swing right, and snake my way past that tree without scraping fiberglass or ripping off a mirror. I looked at the angle, looked at the tree, looked back at the angle, and decided, *Nope*.

There's brave, and then there's foolish. Attempting that right turn in a 36-foot motorhome was firmly in the "foolish" category.

So, I improvised. Instead of going right, I went left. It wasn't elegant, and it wasn't what the campground map showed, but it was the only option that didn't involve Bertie Bea meeting a tree trunk up close and personal.

* * *

Even then, it wasn't easy. The campground roads were muddy from recent rain, and climbing a hill out of there felt like trying to coax a walrus up a waterslide. I could feel Bertie's tires slipping, mud flying, and my heart racing. Getting stuck in a car is frustrating. Getting stuck in a 24,500-pound motorhome is terrifying. Tow trucks for rigs like Bertie Bea don't just magically appear—they take hours, sometimes days, and they don't come cheap.

But somehow, through sheer determination and maybe a little divine intervention, we made it. Bertie clawed her way up the hill, mud splattering, engine roaring, and finally emerged onto solid ground. I let out a breath I didn't realize I'd been holding and gave Bertie an affectionate pat on the dashboard.

We were free.

Now, I try not to be the guy who leaves negative reviews. Every campground has its quirks, and most of the time, a smile and a little patience go a long way. But this? This had to be documented. I left a fairly negative review explaining exactly what happened: that I'd been parked in what seemed like the smallest site in the entire campground, that the roads were muddy enough to make me question whether I should've brought snow chains in May, and that calling it a "pull-through" was a stretch at best. I figured future RVers deserved a heads-up before finding themselves in the same predicament.

Once we were back on the highway, the tension finally eased. Rosie was back in her place, Bertie was humming along, and I could already feel the story turning into one of those "laugh about it later" tales. But make no mistake: in the moment, it was a highlight of the Summer RV Tour 2023 in the worst way possible.

And the funny part? I thought that was going to be the big parking nightmare of the trip. Little did I know, Washington State and a driveway at Loon Lake would soon show me what *real* postage stamp parking looked like. Compared to that, Big Timber was just a warm-up.

Still, I walked away from Big Timber with a new appreciation for planning ahead and double-checking site photos when possible. Because in RV life, "pull-through" doesn't always mean "easy." Sometimes it means "you'll pull through this if you survive."

CHAPTER SIX

Jackpots and Tight Turns

If there's one thing RV life teaches you quickly, it's that turning right is never as simple as it looks. In a normal car, you swing the wheel, cut the corner, and move on with your life. In a 36-foot motorhome towing a car, every right turn is an event. It's geometry in motion, a rolling math problem where the stakes involve curb rash, dented rims, or Rosie hopping the curb like a stunt driver who missed her calling in a demolition derby.

I learned this the hard way.

The first time I jumped a curb with Rosie faithfully in tow, I didn't even realize what had happened until I heard the telltale *thunk* and felt the tug from behind. In my mind, I'd made the turn perfectly. Smooth, steady, no problem. But the reality was that while Bertie Bea had cleared the corner, Rosie was doing her best Evel Knievel impression in the rearview camera. Thankfully, she came out of it with nothing more than a scuffed tire, but it was enough to make my heart stop.

Right turns are tricky because the pivot point on a motorhome isn't where you think it is. Your brain wants to drive it like a car, but your car doesn't have a wheelbase long enough to host a square dance. Add in a tow bar and a car behind you, and suddenly your rear end swings wide like a barn door. What clears for the motorhome doesn't always clear for the toad. And what doesn't clear? Well, Rosie has the curb rash to prove it.

And it's not just campgrounds. Gas stations, grocery store parking lots, casinos—you name it, I've probably had a too-tight right turn there. RV life is full of these moments where you find yourself in a spot designed for Honda Civics and wonder why in the world you thought squeezing in a 55-foot setup was a good idea.

But campgrounds are where it gets especially hairy. Picture it: you're pulling in after a long day on the road, tired, maybe a little hangry, and all you want to do is get parked and leveled so you can relax. You see the entrance, make the turn, and suddenly realize the radius is about half what you need. Too late. You're committed. And in that moment, you're praying you don't take out the sign at the front gate or put Rosie in the bushes.

That's exactly what happened to me at one campground. One second I was congratulating myself on arriving in one piece, and the next I was holding my breath as Rosie hopped the curb behind me. It wasn't catastrophic—no bent axles, no broken glass—but it was enough of a scare to etch the lesson permanently into my brain: wide turns only, no exceptions.

Casinos haven't been much kinder. They may advertise "RV parking," but what they don't mention is that their entrances are often designed for compact sedans sneaking in for a quick blackjack session. Try muscling a Class A with a toad into those narrow, landscaped driveways, and suddenly the jackpot isn't inside at the slots—it's getting out without ripping your bumper off.

Since that first big scare, I've learned. Now, whenever I approach a right turn into a campground, parking lot, or even a wide-open intersection, I leave myself room. Lots of room. If it feels like I'm swinging out into the next county, good—that means Rosie's wheels have a fighting chance of staying on the pavement.

It sounds obvious now, but when you're new to RVing, your brain is still wired for car turns. You forget that Bertie Bea's wheelbase is long enough to need its own zip code. And while learning this lesson didn't cost me much more than a scuffed tire and some bruised pride, it easily could have gone worse.

That's the theme of this chapter: how my lack of thinking ahead during a few of those tight turns could've ended badly, but thankfully didn't. You'll hear about Rosie's curb-jumping antics, the stress of navigating into tight campgrounds, and yes, the casino parking lot where I nearly donated my bumper to landscaping.

Because here's the thing: RV life will test your patience in big ways—slides failing, storms rolling through, black tanks refusing to cooperate. But sometimes it's the simple right-hand turn that humbles you the most. And if you're not paying attention, you just might find yourself playing a game of roulette with your rig.

Boomtown Casino RV Park: Playing Roulette with a Right Turn

If there's one truth about RV life, it's this: the moments that look easy on paper are usually the ones that give you gray hair. Take a narrow gas station, a tight campground entrance, or a right-hand turn with a toad in tow. None of them sound particularly scary until you find yourself mid-turn, praying you don't hear the gut-wrenching sound of fiberglass scraping against a post.

That was me in March 2025, rolling into Biloxi, Mississippi, on my way back toward Kick Back Ranch & Event Center. I had booked a one-night stay at the Boomtown Casino RV Park. The plan was simple—meet up with friends, catch up over dinner, sleep the night away, and roll on. Easy.

Except, of course, it wasn't.

The Boomtown Casino RV Park is tucked off a side street in Biloxi, and the approach is less "welcoming boulevard" and more "urban obstacle course." The street itself was narrow enough that I kept waiting for someone to pop out with a tape measure to confirm if Bertie Bea and Rosie were even allowed in. Add in oncoming traffic and a tight right-hand turn into the park, and suddenly this wasn't a leisurely cruise into an overnight stop. It was geometry, patience, and luck all colliding in one move.

I had two options: stop well back, swing wide, and make the turn gracefully—or do what I actually did, which was pull up too close and too far to the right, leaving myself almost no room to maneuver. Let's just say I didn't exactly set myself up for success.

As soon as I started the turn, I knew I was in trouble. The angle was wrong, the lane too narrow, and Rosie was faithfully swinging wide behind me like a dance partner trying desperately to follow the lead. Out of the corner of my eye, I saw the fence on one side and the signpost on the other, both closing in like the jaws of a trap.

The dashcams in both Bertie Bea and Rosie caught the whole ordeal. If you watch the footage, you can practically see me sweating through the screen. The tires cleared by inches—*inches*. I came close enough to that fence that I could've reached out the window and picked splinters. And the sign? Let's just say the sign and I became very well acquainted that day.

By some miracle, I made it through without leaving a Bertie Bea–sized scar on Boomtown's property. Once inside, the contrast was almost comical. After that harrowing turn, the RV park itself opened up into a wide, spacious lot with plenty of long pull-through sites. Bertie Bea and Rosie could finally breathe again, stretched out comfortably with room to spare.

That's the irony of RV life. Sometimes the hardest part isn't the driving, the weather, or the setup—it's the 30 feet between the road and the actual campsite. You spend hours cruising down highways, through rainstorms and wind, only to be defeated by a poorly designed entrance that feels like it was created by someone who thought RVs peaked at 20 feet long.

Now, I know what you're thinking: "Stan, why didn't you just stop, reset, and make the turn properly?" Great question. In the moment, though, with traffic stacking up behind me, locals glaring from their steering wheels, and that stubborn voice in my head saying, *You've got this*, I convinced myself to keep going. Spoiler alert: I did not, in fact, "got this."

Looking back, it was pure casino roulette. You roll into Biloxi thinking the gamble is inside at the blackjack tables or the roulette wheel. Nope. The real gamble is whether you'll clear the fence and the sign without leaving half your paint behind. That turn was my spin of the wheel, and the odds weren't great. This time, the ball landed on my number. Next time? Who knows.

Because here's the truth: in Biloxi, the casinos always win. And when it comes to RV entrances, so do the curbs, fences, and posts. You might think you're clever, skilled, and seasoned, but one bad angle and suddenly you're shelling out thousands to fix bent aluminum or cracked fiberglass.

And fiberglass doesn't negotiate. It doesn't care that you were tired, that the traffic was heavy, or that you were just trying to meet friends for dinner. Fiberglass plays by casino rules: the house always wins.

Once I got parked and calmed down, I replayed the dashcam footage. Watching it later, safely inside with the AC humming and Rosie resting comfortably out front, I couldn't help but laugh. There I was, creeping through the turn like I was threading a needle with a garden hose, muttering words that would make a sailor blush, and somehow pulling it off. Comedy gold—if you weren't the guy behind the wheel.

But it also gave me perspective. That one turn taught me a valuable lesson I carry with me everywhere now: when approaching a tight right-hand entrance, don't be afraid to stop, back up traffic, and set yourself up for success. Swing wide. Own the road. Take the space you need, because the alternative is far more costly. Embarrassment fades, but repairs don't.

The rest of my stay at Boomtown was fine. The sites really were nice—long, level, plenty of room to stretch out. The casino was there if I wanted it, though honestly I felt like I'd already had my fill of gambling for the day. My jackpot was escaping that entrance unscathed.

As I packed up to leave the next morning, I made myself a promise: no more rushing turns. If it meant taking up both lanes of traffic for a minute, so be it. If it meant frustrating the guy behind me in his pickup truck, well, he could wait. Because at the end of the day, I'm not driving a Honda Civic—I'm driving Bertie Bea and towing Rosie, and together we take up a lot of space.

* * *

RV life will always come with its share of risks. Storms, black tank disasters, mechanical gremlins—you name it, I've seen it. But sometimes, it's that one right-hand turn into a casino RV park that reminds you just how thin the line can be between smooth sailing and an insurance claim.

And that's why this story sticks with me. Because while I might not have hit the slots or played a hand of poker that night, I still walked away with a lesson worth more than any jackpot: in RV life, the gamble isn't inside the casino—it's the driveway out front.

CHAPTER SEVEN
Rosie vs. the Wyoming Cable

Rosie vs Cable in Wyoming

Road hazards are the great equalizer. It doesn't matter if you're in a Honda Civic, a jacked-up F-250, or a 36-foot motorhome dragging a tow car behind like a tail on a kite—one stray object in the road can turn your day into a country song.

In a car, a hazard is an inconvenience. You blow a tire, bend a rim, maybe limp to the nearest repair shop while muttering under your breath. Painful, sure, but survivable without raiding your retirement fund.

In an RV? Oh, no. Entirely different ballgame. One bad hit can shred your tires, crumple your fiberglass, twist your axles, rip out undercarriage wiring, or take a slide clean out of commission. That innocent-looking hunk of junk lying on the asphalt can morph into a five-figure problem before you've even had time to say, *"Did I hit that?"*

And that's the dirty little secret of RV life: road hazards aren't "maybe" events. They're *inevitable*. Somewhere between Point A and Point B, you're going to meet one. Could be a chunk of semi tire big enough to qualify as modern art. Could be a forgotten two-by-four with nails sticking up like caltrops. Could be rebar, a ladder, or—if you're in cattle country—a very annoyed bovine. And if you're towing a car, the odds double. If Bertha clears it, Rosie's gonna find it. That's just math.

The Cable in the Road

That's exactly what happened to me in Wyoming.

* * *

I was rolling west in Bertha, my 2015 Forest River Sunseeker 3200, Rosie faithfully dancing along behind me on the tow bar. Wyoming highways are deceptive—they lull you into a false sense of security. You get those big skies, the endless stretches of pavement, the kind of scenery that makes you feel like you're driving through a car commercial. Traffic? Practically nonexistent. It's just you, the horizon, and the occasional pronghorn that looks at you like you're lost.

It's easy to forget that danger can appear out of nowhere. Almost.

Because right there, stretched across the asphalt like it owned the place, was a high-tensile strength steel cable.

Cable across the Road in Wyoming

I don't know where it came from. Maybe it slipped off a rancher's truck. Maybe someone's fence had given up on its job and decided the middle of the highway was a better retirement plan. Maybe the road just spawned it out of spite. All I know is it wasn't supposed to be there.

Bertha rolled over it first. Heavy, solid, no problem. For a brief second, I thought we were in the clear. But then came Rosie. Poor Rosie, innocent and unsuspecting, barreling along right into trouble.

When Two Seconds Feels Like Forever

* * *

Here's the thing: in a car, you might swerve. But in a 24,000-pound Class C with a tow bar and car hooked up? Swerving is a death wish. One wrong move, and you're fishtailing into next week. I had about two seconds to decide: hit the brakes and risk someone rear-ending me at 70 mph, or keep rolling and hope for the best.

I kept rolling.

And then Rosie met the cable.

The sound alone could've been a horror movie trailer: *metallic scrape, thunk, wrap*. It was the unmistakable sound of something expensive about to happen. I felt it tug, heard it clatter, and immediately knew: *Not good. Not good at all.*

When I pulled over to assess the damage, the picture wasn't pretty. Bertha had lost one of her leveling jack cables, dangling like a loose nerve. Rosie had it worse. That steel cable had wrapped itself snugly around her tire and brake, clinging like it was auditioning for a boa constrictor role in a wildlife documentary.

Middle of Nowhere

If there's a phrase that sums up that day, it's "middle of nowhere." Wyoming has a lot of those. Cell signal? Barely. Traffic? Nonexistent. Help? Hours away.

* * *

Cable attached to Bertha and Rosie

Four and a half hours, to be exact. That's how long I waited for roadside assistance to find us. If you've never sat on the shoulder of a lonely highway in Wyoming for that long, let me tell you: it's an experience. The sun moves more slowly, the pronghorn judge harder, and every truck that blows by makes you wonder if the cable's going to yank Rosie's axle clean off before help arrives.

* * *

A cable wrapped around the axle of Rosie

When the tow truck finally appeared, it was like the cavalry arriving over the hill. The driver hopped out, took one look, and said, "Well, that's a first." Not exactly comforting words, but at least he was game. Thirty minutes later, the cable was untangled, cut, and disposed of properly so the next poor soul wouldn't relive my nightmare.

I thanked him, paid the bill, and promised myself I'd add "random cable in the road" to my growing list of RV hazards. Right between "tree limbs taller than they look" and "gas station curbs that leap out of nowhere."

But Wait—There's More

You'd think that would be the end of my bad day. But RV life loves a sequel.

By the time we finally rolled into the campground, it was dark. And if you've never tried navigating a campground after sunset, imagine playing mini-golf blindfolded. Every turn looks the same, every rock looks bigger, and every tree branch suddenly seems like it's aiming for your roof vents.

***

Sure enough, I missed a turn inside the park and nearly clipped a rock the size of Rosie herself. One more foot and I'd have added "boulder damage" to the day's tally. I parked, leveled, and collapsed into the driver's seat with the kind of exhaustion only RVers know.

Lessons from a Cable

That day taught me a handful of lessons I'll never forget.

First: you can't predict hazards, but you can prepare for them. Keep your eyes on the road, leave space, and never assume that just because the highway looks clear, it is.

Second: patience is everything. Four and a half hours on the shoulder isn't fun, but it beats rushing into a bad decision and making things worse.

Third: never, ever trust night parking after a stressful day. Just stop early. It's better to miss a few miles than to miss your front bumper.

Most importantly? I learned that RV life isn't about avoiding problems. It's about surviving them, laughing about them later, and filing them under "campfire stories."

Roulette on the Highway

The truth is, driving an RV is like spinning a roulette wheel. Most days, the ball lands on your number: smooth road, easy drive, uneventful arrival. But every now and then, it hits double zero, and you're untangling a steel cable from your toad in the middle of Wyoming.

The house always wins. On the road, the "house" is the curb, the fence, the rock, or—in my case—that steel cable. And when it wins, it takes your time, your money, and a chunk of your sanity.

But here's the silver lining: I walked away with a story. Rosie survived, Bertha got patched, and I gained another reminder that this lifestyle isn't just about sunsets and campfires. It's about rolling with whatever the road throws at you—even if what it throws is a high-tensile steel cable.

And when I tell the story now, I don't shudder. I laugh. Because if you can't find humor in a day like that, you'll never last in the RV life.

CHAPTER EIGHT
Conclusion: Smooth Roads Ahead (Mostly)

The RV life is fraught with dangers both real and imagined, and yet the trip is always worth the problems you may have when traveling the highways and byways of this great country. If you've made it this far with me, you've heard my share of mishaps, mistakes, and misadventures. And as I sit here reflecting on all of them—the bent awning arms, the black tank blues, the Wyoming cable fiasco, and every postage stamp parking job that made me sweat through my shirt—I realize something important: the gaffes are often the best part of the story.

Nobody sits around the campfire and tells tales about the perfect drive. You'll never hear, *"Remember that day when everything went smoothly? Man, what a ride that was!"* No. The stories worth retelling are the ones where you nearly lost your awning to a gate post in Texas, or you forgot to let the rain drain before pulling in your slide in Louisiana, or you had to call roadside assistance because Rosie met her match in Wyoming steel cable.

Why? Because those are the stories that stick. Those are the ones that turn into laughter years later, when the panic and frustration have faded, leaving only the absurdity. They're the proof that you lived it, survived it, and can now laugh about it.

The Truth About RV Life

People scrolling through Instagram see the sunsets. The mountain views. The pristine campsites with string lights and Adirondack chairs staged just so. And sure, those moments exist—I've had plenty of them myself. But that's only half the story. The other half is what this book has been about: the breakdowns, the boneheaded mistakes, the storms, the parking nightmares, and the unplanned adventures that come with hauling your house down the highway.

RV life isn't about perfection. It's about resilience. It's about realizing that even when the day goes sideways—and believe me, some days will—it doesn't mean the lifestyle isn't worth it. If anything, it makes it more worth it, because you learn to take the good with the bad, and to laugh at yourself when things don't go according to plan.

What I've Learned

Over the years, I've learned a few truths that keep me rolling.

First, patience is your best tool. It's more important than duct tape, more important than a socket set, and yes, even more important than that bottle of Calgon Bath Pearls you keep for the black tank. If you can be patient when you're parking, patient when you're waiting for roadside assistance, patient when your slide decides to quit during a thunderstorm, you'll make it. Impatience, on the other hand, will break more than your mood—it'll break your rig.

Second, the checklist is gospel. I've learned this the hard way—more than once. Forgetting one step, whether it's bringing in the awning or draining the rainwater off a slide topper, can cost you. The checklist isn't optional. It's salvation.

Third, people are part of the journey. From the friends who use three-quarters of a roll of toilet paper in one go, to the strangers who wave frantically trying to warn you that your awning is still out, to the roadside assistance guys who shrug and say, "Well, that's a first"—the cast of characters makes the story richer. RV life isn't a solo act. It's a community, and often the best memories come not from the places, but from the people you meet along the way.

And finally: humor is non-negotiable. If you can't laugh at yourself when you're standing under your awning in the rain, soaked to the bone while jabbing a Lippert reset button with needle-nose pliers, then maybe this lifestyle isn't for you. But if you can laugh? If you can chuckle through the frustration and turn it into a story for later? Then you've got what it takes.

Why It's All Worth It

For every mishap I've shared in these pages, there have been dozens of incredible moments. Quiet mornings by a lake with Rosie parked beside me. Evenings under the stars in the high plains, where the Milky Way looks close enough to touch. Fishing trips with friends on rivers that run clear and fast. Sunsets that light the sky on fire, and sunrises that remind you why you got on the road in the first place.

Would I trade those for never having to deal with another clogged black tank sensor, another narrow driveway, another questionable gas station turn? Not a chance. Because the mishaps are part of the price of admission. They're the toll you pay to live a life of freedom, adventure, and stories worth telling.

And the truth is, most of the time, the rewards outweigh the risks. For every day you're stuck waiting on roadside assistance, there are ten where you're gliding down the highway, coffee in hand, music on the radio, and the horizon wide open in front of you.

Passing It On

So if you're reading this book wondering whether the RV life is for you, here's my advice: don't wait until you think you're ready. You'll never know it all, and you'll never be fully prepared. At some point, you just have to get behind the wheel, point your rig toward the horizon, and go. Mistakes will happen. Things will break. You'll have days where you wonder what in the world you were thinking. But you'll also have days that feel like pure magic, days that make you grateful for the journey, and nights where you sit by the fire and think, *This is exactly where I'm supposed to be.*

The Road Ahead

As for me, I know there are still plenty of bumps, blunders, and belly laughs waiting up ahead. More storms, more parking nightmares, more surprises from Rosie. But that's okay. Because I've learned that the road will never stop teaching me. And as long as Bertie Bea, Rosie, and I keep rolling, there will always be another story to tell.

So here's to the road—messy, unpredictable, and wonderful. Here's to the mistakes that make the best memories. And here's to finding humor in the hazards, because without it, you'll miss the very best part of the ride.

Smooth roads ahead… most of the time.

www.ingramcontent.com/pod-product-compliance
Lightning Source LLC
LaVergne TN
LVHW022013080426
835513LV00009B/696